GW01238331

The Old Fashione(

More Gags in the Classic Stand-Up Style

Compiled by Hugh Morrison

Montpelier Publishing

London

2015

ISBN-13: 978-1516822591

ISBN-10: 1516822595

Published by Montpelier Publishing, London.

Printed by Amazon Createspace.

My father gave most of his money to sick animals. The trouble was, he didn't know they were sick when he betted on them.

'Is your wife outspoken?'

'Not by anyone I know.'

'It's our fortieth wedding anniversary next week my dear,' said a man to his wife. 'What would you like as a present? A diamond necklace, a car, a world cruise?'

'I want a divorce,' said his wife.

'I wasn't planning on spending that much,' replied the man.

Scoutmaster: What's the best way to start a fire with two sticks?

Scout: Make sure one of them is a match.

My girlfriend dumped me because she didn't like my records. To this day I've still no idea how she got them from my doctor and probation officer.

An elderly couple had dinner at another couple's house, and after eating, the wives left the table and went into the kitchen. The two elderly gentlemen were talking, and one said, 'Last night we went

1

out to a new restaurant, and it was really great. I would recommend it very highly.'

The other man said, 'What's the name of the restaurant?' The first man thought hard, and finally said to his companion, 'What's the name of that red flower you give to someone you love?' His friend replied, 'A carnation?' 'No. No. The other one,' the man said. The other man offered another suggestion, 'A geranium?' 'No, said the man. 'You know the one that's red and has thorns.'

His friend said, 'Do you mean a rose?' 'Yes, yes that's it. Thank you!' the first man said. He then turned towards the kitchen and yelled, 'Rose, what's the name of that restaurant we went to last night?'

'I took my wife on holiday to Bulgaria.'

'Sofia?'

'No, Maureen.'

'Is she a natural blonde or a platinum blonde?'

'Neither. She's a suicide blonde.'

'A suicide blonde? What's that?'

'Dyed by her own hand.'

Two students were talking. 'My father's offered to give me £5000 if I give up all my bad habits,' said one. 'Why do you look so unhappy then?' said his friend. 'Well,' said the other, 'if I give up all my bad habits, what am I going to spend £5000 on?'

Letter to agony aunt: 'I am a seventeen year old girl. Last night I stayed out very late with a boy and my mother was angry when I got home. Did I do wrong?'

Reply: 'Try to remember!'

Don't ask me,

'Is that a popular song he's singing?'

'It was before he sang it.'

'My wife is the most wonderful woman in the world – and that's not just my opinion, it's hers as well!'

'I came home drunk last night and my wife had changed the locks.'

'That's terrible.'

'It gets worse. She'd changed the street we live on as well!'

Complaint to railway company: 'I was disgusted to find that the so-called "quiet carriage" on your trains makes the same annoying "diddly dum, diddly dee" noise as all the rest of them.'

They say prostitution is the world's oldest profession. If that's true, how did the men earn the money to pay for it?

'ɔpare some change, guv?'

'Sorry, I don't have any.'

'Aw go on. Just a few pence.'

'Really, I haven't any.'

'What do you want me to do? Beg for it?'

Paddy was getting married and realised he didn't have much experience with women. He went to a bookshop and bought a book entitled 'How to Hug.' Only three weeks later did he realise it was Volume 7 of the Encyclopaedia Britannica.

Doctor: (to elderly patient) How's your sex life?

Patient: Not bad. I have sex almost every day.

Doctor: Really?

Patient: Yes. Almost on Monday...almost on Tuesday...almost on Wednesday...

I love my wife terribly. Well, that's what she tells me anyway.

The teacher was explaining about vowels and consonants. 'Can anyone remember what the two kinds of letter in the alphabet are called?' Little Johnny put up his hand. 'Big ones and small ones.'

'I told my wife not to spend so much, but I got a sob story.'

'You mean she cried?'

'No, she just called me an S.O.B.'

The train was about to leave and the guard blew his whistle. 'Wait a minute!' called a young feminine voice. 'I'm still trying to get my clothes off!' All male eyes turned to the door, only to see a woman struggling to lift a large laundry bag onto the platform.

An Englishman was on a walking holiday in Spain. He arrived at a small cafe in the country where he ordered tea. The tea arrived without milk. 'I can't possibly drink tea without milk,' thought the man; but he spoke no Spanish and the waiter spoke no English.

After trying to make the waiter understand what he wanted without success, inspiration struck the man and he drew a picture of a cow on a paper napkin.

The waiter smiled, nodded, and left the cafe. Twenty minutes later he came back with a ticket for a bullfight.

Daughter: Mother, what kind of husband should I look for?

Mother: You leave the husbands alone, and look for a single man!

Have you ever felt like going into an antique shop and saying 'what's new?'

Man proposes, but divorce exposes.

'Where have you been?'

'To the cemetery'.

'Good Lord – is somebody dead?'

'Yes, all of them.'

'I don't mind having my mother in law live with us. But I do wish she'd wait until we get married!'

Paddy and Seamus were running a race to a tree, by different routes. 'If I get there first,' said Paddy, 'I'll make a mark on the tree with this chalk. If you get there first, you rub it off.'

Passenger on cruise ship (to steward): Is my wife forward?

Steward: Not with me, sir.

'My father made his fortune with his pen.'

'Oh really? Poetry or prose?'

'Neither – he was a pig farmer.'

He: You girls look much shorter in those bikinis.

She: Yes, and you men look much longer!

Admiral (to sailor): Are you a family man?

Sailor: Yes sir, I've got a wife and six children.

Admiral: Really. Don't you ever get homesick?

Sailor: Only when I'm at home, sir.

'Well I'll be damned,' said the river as the fat lady fell off the bridge.

An aspiring novelist sent a manuscript to a publisher with a covering note which read 'The characters in this story are purely fictional and bear no resemblance to anyone, living or dead.' A few days later the manuscript was returned. The editor had written on the note: 'That's what's wrong with it.'

They say 'ignorance of the law is no defence.' Unless you're a lawyer.

'She told me that you told her what I told you not to tell her.'

'I told her not to tell you I told her.'

'Oh dear. Well, don't tell her I told you that she told me.'

A hypochondriac told his doctor that he had a serious kidney disease. 'Nonsense,' said the doctor. 'You wouldn't know if you had that — there are no symptoms until it's too late.' The patient replied, 'I know — that's why I'm worried I might have it.'

McTavish dreamt one night that he'd lent a man a hundred pounds. The next night, he was too afraid to go to sleep in case he dreamt he hadn't been paid back.

Seamus: I bet ye can't eat five pounds o'potatoes in one sittin'.

Paddy: Sure and I can. But only if they're small ones!

Prison chaplain (to convict): My good man, I hope you have realised the error of your ways.

Convict: I certainly have, padre. Next time, I'll wear gloves!

'We must learn to be satisfied with what we have,' said the vicar to one of his poor parishioners. 'Oh I am vicar,' said the man, 'it's what I haven't got that I'm dissatisfied with.'

Small boy (to father): Here's my report card. And just for reference, here's one of yours I found in the attic.

Curate (to vicar): Does your wife embroider church kneelers?

Vicar: No, but I'm told she adorned numerous pillows before I met her.

She: Did you ask my father for my hand in marriage?

He: Yes, I did it on the telephone.

She: What did he say?

He: 'I don't know who you are, but it's alright.'

A woman invested some money in a company which went bust. With great shame she told her husband of the loss of five hundred pounds.

'My dear,' said the man sadly, 'didn't I tell you always to consult me about whether to make an investment?'

'You did,' replied his wife.

'So why didn't you ask me?'

'I was worried you'd tell me not to.'

Judge (to defendant): Do you plead guilty or not guilty?

Defendant: I thought that's what you lot were supposed to find out!

A woman answered a knock at the door. 'Yes?' she said to the stranger standing there. 'Piano tuner, ma'am,' replied the man. 'But I didn't ask you to come,' said the woman. 'Besides, I can't afford to pay.' 'No problem ma'am,' said the man. 'The neighbours sent me and they paid in advance.'

Husband: Why don't we go south for the winter?

Wife: What for? We've got all the winter we need right here!

A tramp knocked on the door of a country cottage and asked for food. 'Come around to the back door,' said the lady of the house. The 'gentleman of the road' did so, but as he was about to enter the back garden, he noticed a bulldog in the corner. 'Will the dog bite?' said the tramp warily. 'I don't know,' said the woman. 'I've just bought him this morning and I'd like to find out.'

'My sister's just become a duchess.'

'Really – did she marry a duke?'

'No, a Dutchman.'

Woman (in photographer's studio): I wish to complain about wedding photos you took. My husband looks like an ape!

Photographer: Well you should have thought of that before you married him!

'Did the doctor really mean it when he said you wouldn't live a week if you didn't stop chasing women?'

'He certainly did – I've been chasing his wife!'

Wife (to husband): Can you buy me a mousetrap?

Husband: I bought you one yesterday.

Wife: Yes, but that one's got a mouse in it.

'I see Jane's burning the candle at both ends again.'

'How?'

'Last week it was her birthday and she had 21 candles on the cake.'

'How do you know that he married her for her money?'

'I've seen her!'

'Why are you so late coming home?' said a woman to her drunken husband at midnight. 'Well my dear, you told me to walk straight back from the pub,' replied the man. 'I did,' said his wife angrily, 'but the pub closes at eleven. What have you been doing since then?' 'Waiting until I could walk straight,' replied the man.

Two elderly men were discussing their wives. 'My wife's gone, but not forgotten,' said one. The other sighed. 'My wife hasn't gone...and she hasn't forgotten either.'

They say a woman's work is never done. They're lucky. If a man's work was never done, he'd get the sack.

'My husband's no good at fixing things. So everything in our house works.'

'My wife's worried about having thirteen people to dinner tonight.'

'Superstitious, eh?'

'No, we've only got twelve matching plates.'

'I remember the days when we all left our back doors unlocked,' recalled the elderly man. 'We weren't more honest; it's just that

12

whenever anyone stole anything, we could always get it back, as the thieves always left their back doors open as well.'

Angry father: When I die, I shall leave you without a penny.

Son: Quite right. You can't take it with you!

Waiter: Dogs are not allowed in this restaurant, sir.

Man: That's not my dog.

Waiter: But he's following you.

Man: Well, so are you!

Man (on phone to doctor) Come quickly – my wife's about to have a baby!

Doctor: I'll come right away. Fetch lots of towels and boiling water.

Man: Why?

Doctor: Because it's raining outside and I'd like a cup of tea when I arrive.

The chief of a tribe of cannibals was asked why he had given up eating people. 'The British kept sending missionaries,' he explained, 'and you can't keep a good man down.'

Medium: The spirit of your wife wishes to speak with you.

Widower: You're a fake! My wife would never ask permission to speak with me!

'Would you like to buy a raffle ticket sir? First prize is a week's holiday in Margate.'

'What's the second prize?'

'Two weeks' holiday in Margate.'

In the Great War an Irish regiment were marching through Belgium. Private O'Riley, half dead with hunger, saw a plump chicken by the side of the road and broke ranks to run after it. The commanding officer noticed and shouted 'Halt!' O' Riley ignored him and continued chasing the chicken. 'Halt I say!' screamed the officer, going red in the face. Finally O'Riley caught the chicken, and in front of the officer wrung its neck. 'There,' said O'Riley. 'That'll teach you to halt when the officer tells ye!'

Chemistry professor: What can you tell me about nitrates?

Student: They're cheaper than day rates.

A football manager was being interviewed after a match. 'I promised the lads we'd either win, lose, or draw, and I didn't let them down.'

'My wife and I have only argued once in ten years of marriage.'

'Remarkable.'

'Not really. See that scar?'

A vicar asked a man in his parish why he never attended church. 'Every time you go there somebody throws something on you,' said the man. Confused, the vicar asked what he meant. 'The first time you go they throw water on you, the second time they throw confetti on you, and the third time they throw earth on you.'

Two men were walking home late from the pub. 'What will you say to your wife?' asked one. 'Nothing,' replied the other. 'She usually thinks of something.'

Daughter: I want a husband who is easily pleased.

Mother: Don't worry dear. That's probably the kind you'll get.

She: Did you get a commission in the army?

He: No, just a basic salary.

'I see Jane's turned 35. When is she thinking of getting married?'

'Constantly.'

The British ambassador was to give an after- dinner speech in China. The room was full of Chinese politicians, none of whom could speak English. Hoping to break the ice before his speech, he told a long joke. When he'd finished the interpreter said one sentence and everyone in the room burst into loud laughter. Afterwards the ambassador asked the interpreter how he'd managed to sum up the joke so briefly. 'I didn't,' he explained. 'I just said "the ambassador has just told a joke. Everybody please laugh."'

'They do argue over trifles but I'm not sure that's such a bad sign.'

'How so?'

'It may mean they don't have anything else to argue about.'

'You're not just marrying that man for his money, are you?'

'Of course not. It's the little things about him that I like.'

'Such as?'

'Oh, his little place in the country, his little flat in town, his little private island...'

'Darling, in this moonlight your teeth are like pearls.'

'Oh really – and since when have you been in the moonlight with Pearl?'

She: You remind me of the sea.

He: What? Wild, restless and romantic?

She: No, you make me sick.

A burglar who is working too hard could do with arrest.

A woman in a top floor flat dialled 999 and asked to speak to the fire brigade. 'My husband's gone out and locked my bedroom door, and now a man's trying to get in through my window,' she said, with a trembling voice. 'This is the fire brigade,' said the voice on the line. 'You need the police.' 'No I don't,' said the woman. 'You're the ones with the ladder.'

Little Johnny: We're getting another room put on our house.

Little Jimmy: That's nothing. I heard my dad say we're getting another mortgage on ours!

Intuition: the strange instinct that tells a woman she's right, whether she is or not.

It was amateur night at a Glasgow music hall and a pretentious poet, with anguished face, began to declaim a poem in a mournful voice from the stage. 'Alone, alone, all, all alone!' 'Aye,' shouted a heckler from the audience, 'and no bloody wonder!'

Wife: I'm looking at this chart from the doctor to find out if my height-to-weight ratio is correct.

Husband: And is it?

Wife: No – according to this I should be six inches taller.

Little Johnny was locked in his room. 'Now don't let me catch you stealing biscuits from the kitchen again,' said his mother. 'Well,' replied the boy tearfully 'I tried not to let you catch me *this* time.'

Vicar (collecting in the street): My mission is to save prostitutes.

Drunk: Tha's great rev'rend. Could yer save a couple for me too?

Man (to in-laws visiting): Is there anything I can get you? Tea? Coffee? Hats and coats?

Traveller (in railway buffet): Are these stale buns all you have to eat?

Bored waitress: I don't have to eat them – you do.

Prison visitor (to convict): Why are you here, my good man?

Convict: I'm the victim of unlucky number thirteen.

Prison visitor: How so?

Convict: Twelve jurors and a judge.

'I have a foolproof method to promote hair growth.'

'What's that?'

'Stop having it cut.'

An agony aunt was asked by a young lady how to get rid of unwanted hair on the upper lip. 'Push the young man away' was the reply.

An Australian visitor to England was asked what he thought of Shakespeare. 'No idea, mate,' came the reply. 'I prefer Foster's beer.'

Nurse: Doctor, a patient has collapsed in the surgery and we can't get her back up.

Doctor: Well see if you can get any other part of her up!

Foreman: You know you're not supposed to smoke while you're working.

Labourer: Who says I'm working?

Mrs Jones had just got her driving licence and was proudly giving her non-driving friend Mrs Brown a lift. She stopped at a red light, took out her compact and powdered her nose. 'Shouldn't you be looking at the traffic light?' asked her friend. 'Oh I don't need to,' said Mrs Jones. 'I just listen for that loud tooting noise it makes.'

Alcohol: an excellent liquid for keeping almost anything – except secrets.

A factory manager put a sign on the shop floor which read 'I want to see everyone happy at their work. Please write below any suggestions that will help bring this about.' The next day somebody had written beneath it: 'Wear noisy shoes.'

Husband: You ought to put something away for a rainy day.

Wife: I have.

Husband: Really – what?

Wife: An umbrella.

Before marriage, men will swear undying love. After marriage, they just swear.

Mrs Smith: My husband buys me a new coat every time it's my birthday.

Mrs Jones: How lovely! You must have an awful lot of coats.

The bereaved relations gathered round to hear the solicitor read the will. 'Being of sound mind...I spent everything before I died.'

If every car in the world were placed end-to-end...it would be the M25.

'The government's told us we all need to tighten our belts. What are you going to do about it?'

'Wear braces.'

A man went into a junk shop and saw an amateurish landscape painting in an old frame. The picture was horrible, but looking more closely, the man noticed that the frame was hallmarked solid silver. 'How much for this old picture?' asked the man. 'Oh that,' said the shopkeeper, 'you can have that for two pounds.' With great excitement the man paid the money. 'The frame's not included though,' said the shop keeper. 'That's ridiculous,' said the man. 'Why on earth can't I have the frame as well?' 'Because,' said the shopkeeper with a smile as he removed the picture, 'that frame's helped me sell 75 pictures.'

McPherson was known as the most parsimonious man in the whole of his small Highland town. One day the minister was out collecting for a new church hall. McPherson refused to donate. 'Everybody's given something but you,' said the minister.

Still the man would not be moved. Eventually inspiration struck the clergyman and he said 'Mr McPherson, if you donate just five pounds, I will display the bank note on the wall of the new hall, with the inscription 'donated by Angus McPherson'.

The canny Scot thought for a moment. 'So you're not going to spend the money, then?' 'No,' said the minister. 'It will be there in perpetuity as an example to all, of your Christian charity.' 'I'll do it,' said McPherson. 'But I'll give ye a cheque instead.'

Wife: I mended that little hole in your jacket pocket for you dear. Aren't you pleased?

Husband: Yes...but how did you know there was a hole in my pocket?

A man attended his wife's funeral, and after the ceremony, the clergyman approached him and said 'My good man; I know that at this time you are sorely grieved; but always remember, there is one who will console you, who shares in your suffering, and who will enfold you in arms of unfailing love.' The man wiped away his tears and said 'That's good to know vicar...what's her name?'

Paterfamilias (about to punish son for lying): When I was your age, my boy, I never told a lie.

Son: What age did you start?

Woman to bank clerk: I wish to make a withdrawal from my husband's part of our joint account.

Molly: That Fred Smith is a terrible ladies' man.

Polly: Why's that?

Molly: Well he's asked me out three times, and I've turned him down every time – and now he's going out with someone else!

McNab invited McTavish over to his house for supper. To McTavish's disgust, McNab took the larger of the two herrings from the dish. 'I don't think much o' your manners,' said McTavish. 'If I'd been in your place I would have taken the smaller fish.' 'Well,' replied McNab, 'You've got it noo.'

Sunday school teacher (to class): Can anyone tell me what we must do before our sins are forgiven?

Little Johnny: Start sinning!

Mother (to son): If you promise not to say 'damn' I'll give you ten pence.

Little Johnny: Alright then. I know another word that's worth at least a pound!

McTavish won the lottery and was so shocked that he collapsed in a dead faint and was ordered to stay in bed by the doctor. His wife instead went to collect the money from the lottery office. The press had heard about the big win, and a reporter thrust a microphone at Mrs McTavish. 'What's the first thing your husband's going to do with the money?' he asked. 'Count it,' she replied.

'My dear McTavish, (said the clergyman) do ye not know that whisky kills more people than road accidents?'

'Maybe so minister, but personally I'd rather be drunk than run over.'

A politician was visiting a lunatic asylum. While being shown around by the supervisor, the visitor said 'That woman over there...is she dangerous?' Glancing towards the woman in question, the supervisor said 'some of the time, yes.' 'But she has such a vicious look about her,' replied the politican. 'Why is she allowed to walk around?' 'Can't help it,' said the supervisor. 'But isn't she under your control?' asked the politician. 'Not really,' replied the supervisor. 'She's my wife.'

Husband: Our little son was so pretty as a baby. But now he's getting uglier every day.'

Wife: Well you didn't expect him to resemble you straight away did you?

Woman (to cleaning lady): That jug you broke yesterday belonged to my great-great-grandmother.

Cleaning lady: Thank heavens for that! I was worried it might be new!

A man passed an old hardware shop called 'The Three Wonders.' Puzzled by what it could mean, he went into the cluttered interior and asked the shopkeeper where the shop's name came from. Without saying a word, the shopkeeper pointed to a sign above the counter:

You wonder if I have it.

I wonder where it is.

Everybody wonders how I find it.

Wife: What do you think of these new shoes? They were free.

Husband: Really? Why were they free?

Wife: Well, they were marked down from £80 to £40, so I bought them with the £40 I saved.

Policeman: Come quietly now. The magistrate will want to see you in the morning.

Prisoner: No he won't. He told me he never wanted to see me before him again.

'It isn't the £25,000 I have in the bank that makes you want to marry me, is it?' said the young woman to her suitor. 'It certainly isn't,' he replied. 'I thought it was much more than that.'

'My wife worships me. She places a burnt offering before me every night.'

Customer (in barber shop): I'd like my hair cut please.

Barber: Certainly sir. Any particular way?

Customer: Yes – off.

A woman saw a man in the street begging, with a sign round his neck which read 'deaf and dumb'. As she put some money in his cup, he said 'thank you.' 'I thought you were supposed to be deaf and dumb,' said the woman indignantly. 'I'm not, missus,' said the man. 'I'm just minding the spot for the bloke until he ge\ 'Oh...alright then,' said the woman. 'But where's he gone   ._ ɔ over there in the pub,' said the man, 'listening to the juke box.'

Tiresome visitor: Do you know, whenever I hear Mozart, I am completely carried away.

Host: What a pity. Our record player is broken.

'I saw you the other night by the docks winking at a woman.'

'I wasn't winking. Something got in my eye.'

'She got in your car as well!'

'Did you hear the story about the two holes in the ground?'

'No.'

'Well, well.'

A Hollywood actor was boring his dinner party companion with tales of his great achievements. 'But enough about me,' said the actor, to the other's great relief. 'What did *you* think of my latest film?'

New post office worker (to old hand): This parcel is marked "fragile". What does that mean?

Old hand: Means throw it underarm.

'I don't find her attractive.'

'Why not?'

'In the first place, she's too fat...and she's too fat in the second place as well!'

Daughter: Do all turkeys have wishbones, mummy?

Mother: Yes dear.

Daughter: Then why don't they all wish that Christmas never comes?

McTavish took his wife to the theatre. They sat in the gallery and Mrs McTavish got so engrossed in the play that she leant too far over the rail and fell into the stalls below. 'For God's sake git up woman,' cried McTavish after her. 'It costs thirty pounds doon there!'

'How long was your last secretary with you?'

'She was never with me – she was against me from the start!'

'Everyone needs to breath oxygen to live. But it was only discovered in 1783,' said the science teacher. Little Johnny put up his hand. 'Please sir,' he asked, 'what did they breath before it was discovered?'

'That man in the pub kept trying to put his hand down my dress.'

'What did you say to him?'

'"Keep it up."'

What is a woman worth? Double you, O man.

Wife (to stingy husband): I don't like our new house.

Husband: Why not?

Wife: There are no curtains in the bathroom. The neighbours can see me taking a bath.

Husband: Why worry? They'll buy their own curtains soon enough!

The judge addressed the court in a sombre voice. 'I received in the post this morning a cheque for ten thousand pounds from the defendant and a cheque for fifteen thousand pounds from the plaintiff. This sort of thing will not be tolerated in my court. The case will be tried strictly on its merits. I have therefore arranged for five thousand pounds to be returned to the plaintiff.'

Fortune teller (to lady): Madam, your future looks black.

Lady: Wait a minute, I've still got my gloves on!

A tourist was visiting the Alps. A guide took him on a long, steep climb to the top of a mountain. 'Look down there,' said the guide. 'Isn't it beautiful down there in that valley?' 'If it's so beautiful down there,' said the tourist breathlessly, 'why the devil did you bring me all the way up here?'

A man went to a restaurant famous for its rude waiters. 'Give me two fried eggs, and a few kind words,' said the man. The waiter brought his order. 'What about the kind words?' said the man. The waiter leant over and whispered, 'Don't eat the eggs.'

Waiter (in fashionable restaurant): How did you find the beef, sir?

Diner: Oh, I just moved a potato, and there it was.

Woman (to shop assistant): Could you take that dress out of the window for me?

Assistant: Certainly madam. Would madam care to try it on?

Woman: No – I just hate seeing it every time I walk past.

McTavish asked for a pint of beer in a pub. The beer didn't fill the glass. 'That's short,' said McTavish. 'No, we just use bigger glasses,' said the barman. McTavish drank the lot in one go. 'That'll be three pounds,' said the barman. McTavish put three fifty pence pieces on the bar. 'Here, this is short,' said the barman. 'Naw,' replied McTavish. 'I just use bigger coins.'

Marriage: the only scientific example of an immovable object co-existing with an irresistable force.

Two elderly gentlemen were talking in their club. 'The other day I dreamt I was addressing the House of Lords,' said one, 'then I woke up – and realised I was!'

Two men were drinking at the club and a third walked in.

'Is that Timkins, the criminal lawyer?'

'Yes,– but nothing's been proven.'

'Daddy, I found this bikini lying on the beach.'

'Well done son. Now come with daddy and show me *exactly* where you found it.'

'Gambling has brought our family closer together.'

'How's that?'

'We've had to buy a smaller house.'

Paddy and Seamus were on a building site arguing about who was the stronger. 'See that wheelbarrow there?' said Paddy. 'I'll bet I can push a load in there that you can't.' 'Go on and fetch it then,' said Seamus, 'and we'll see about that. There isn't a load in the world I can't shift.' Paddy brought the wheelbarrow over and put it in front of Seamus. 'Alright then,' said Paddy. 'Get in.'

'I have a terrible time remembering people's names,' said Smith.

'So do I,' replied Jones, 'but I have a clever way of getting them to repeat it. I just ask "Do you spell your name with an e or an i?" It usually works.'

'I've tried that method before,' said Smith. 'It worked fine until I tried it with Mr Hill.'

'State the amount of coal exported from the United States in any one year,' was a question on the schoolboy's examination paper. He thought for a moment then wrote '1492: none.'

Jones' wife was in the delivery room of the hospital. Terrible groans and cries came from within. When she finally came out with their new baby, Jones said with tears in his eyes, 'my dear, I'm so sorry to have caused you this trouble!' 'Don't worry dear,' replied Mrs Jones. 'I'm sure it wasn't your fault.'

Sign in shop: 'Nothing sold for credit. Not much sold for cash, either.'

'And this, I suppose,' said a man in an art gallery, 'is one of those horrors you call modern art.' 'No sir,' replied the guide. 'That's just a mirror.'

She: When we're married, we ought to have no secrets. You must tell me everything.

He: But...er...I don't know everything!

Little Johnny went into a sweetshop and asked for a bag of jelly babies. 'But I want them all to be boy babies,' said Johnny with a serious expression. The shopkeeper smiled indulgently and asked why. 'More jelly on them,' replied Johnny.

McTavish met his wife at the station after a business trip to London.

'Did ye bring me a present?' asked his wife.

'Aye, I did,' replied McTavish. 'I got ye a souvenir mug.'

'Whit does it say on it?'

'British Rail.'

Judge: Why didn't you attempt to settle this case out of court?

Defendant: That's just what we were doing your honour, until the police came and broke us up.

An American tourist was unimpressed by the masterpieces in the Louvre. 'We've got plenty of priceless paintings in the United States too,' he said. 'I know,' said the guide. 'Van Gogh painted 900 pictures, and America has all ten thousand of them.'

Some people like their work so much, they can just sit and look at it for hours.

'The pianist tonight was wonderful. I hear he learnt to play at four.'

'Four this afternoon?'

At a highland wedding, one of the guests expressed surprise that the collection plate had been passed round during the service. 'Yes it is unusual,' said the church elder, 'but the father of the bride requested it.'

'An astrologer told me not to marry in January if I wanted to avoid trouble. Of course, the same advice holds good for the other eleven months too.'

'I get the hardest part of the day's work done before breakfast.'

'Which part's that?'

'Getting up!'

A rose by any other name would smell as sweet.

A chrysanthemum by any other name would be easier to spell.

A toastmaster was calling out the names of guests as they arrived at a banquet. A prominent local tailor entered and the toastmaster asked his name. 'Don't you remember me?' said the tailor. 'I made your trousers.' 'Ah yes,' said the toastmaster, and solemnly announced: 'Major Trousers.'

First secretary: How's your new boss?

Second secretary: Not bad, but he's a bit narrow minded.

First secretary: How so?

Second secretary: He thinks words can only be spelled one way.

'You say the wedding went off without a hitch?'

'Yes – the chap due to be hitched didn't turn up.'

'I heard a great joke the other day. Perhaps I've told it to you?'

'Is it funny?'

'Yes.'

'Then you haven't.'

Paddy and Seamus visited Rome and went into a bar for some refreshment. Paddy nudged Seamus. 'See that feller over there,' he said, pointing to an elderly gent in the corner, 'sure and I tink that's the Pope.'

'Don't be so stupid,' scoffed Seamus. 'What would the Pope be after doing in a place like this?' 'I'm sure it's him,' protested Paddy. 'Alright, let's ask him,' said Seamus.

They went over. 'Excuse me sir,' said Seamus, 'but we was wondering....' Immediately the man shouted at them in heavily accented English 'Go to hell and leave me alone, damn you!' The two Irishmen went back to their seats. 'What a shame,' said Paddy. 'Now we'll never know!'

A young lothario entered an expensive boutique with his new girlfriend late one Friday afternoon. He told her she could have anything in the shop so she picked out a designer dress priced at £10,000. 'We can't take such a large amount right away, sir', said the assistant, 'but we will put the dress aside until Monday when your bank can confirm the payment.' On Monday the man received a phone call from the shop. 'I'm terribly sorry sir,' said the assistant, 'but the bank has declined the payment. They say you only have £50 in your account.' 'Oh I thought they probably would,' said the man, 'but thanks for a great weekend!'

The teacher wrote a sentence on the blackboard, which read: 'I didn't have no fun at the weekend.'

'Now children, how can I correct this?' she asked.

Little Johnny put up his hand. 'Get yourself a boyfriend, miss!'

A young couple filled their new home with products entirely paid for with coupons cut from cereal packets. They proudly showed their respective parents round the house, pointing out all the gadgets they'd bought. 'There are four rooms in this house and you've only shown us three,' said the woman's mother. 'What's in that other room?' 'Oh that,' replied her daughter. 'That's where we keep all the cereal packets.'

I'm not saying it's a small town, but if you see a girl out with a man old enough to be her father, he probably is.

'I could live on onions and garlic alone.'

'You'd have to.'

A man was travelling on a train from London to Edinburgh and noticed an elderly man in Highland dress get out at every station. Each time he ran madly along the platform, bought a ticket, dashed back and got into the train just in time.

After a while the man became curious, and asked the Scotsman what was going on. 'Weell,' he said, 'I dinnae want to pay for a ticket for the whole journey to Edinburgh.' 'Why on earth not?' asked the Londoner, suspecting foul play.

The Scot explained: 'I've just been told by the doctor I've a heart condition and could drop dead at any moment.'

Book keeping taught in one easy lesson: don't lend them.

23 year old Miss Jones was to be married to 50 year old Mr Brown. 'I'm not sure I understand these "May to December" marriages,' said her mother. 'I can see that he gets a beautiful young woman for "May" but what on earth is the attraction for you in "December"?' The bride to be smiled and replied, 'Christmas.'

There are two reasons why some people don't mind their own business. One is that they haven't any business, and the other is that they haven't any mind.

'Didn't I meet you in Swansea?'

'Don't think so – I've never been to Swansea.'

'Neither have I. It must have been two other fellows.'

At a psychology conference three academics were discussing the topic of prenatal influence. 'When my mother was pregnant with me, she tripped over a dog, and consequently I have a terrible fear of dogs,' said one man.

'When my mother was pregnant with me, she almost fell from a bus; and I have a phobia about public transport.'

'What nonsense,' said the third man. 'When my mother was pregnant with me she collapsed on top of a gramophone. But it didn't affect me...affect me...affect me...affect me...'

Wife: Did you see that lovely hat Mrs Jones was wearing at morning service today?

Husband: Er, no dear. I'm afraid I was asleep most of the time.

Wife: Well really, I don't know why you bother coming to church.

Biology teacher: Can anyone name the parts of the bowels?

Little Johnny: Yes miss. A, E, I, O, U.

Stable owner (to new jockey): Have you ever had an accident while riding?

Jockey: No, sir.

Owner: Then where did you get that scar on your head?

Jockey: Thrown from a horse, sir.

Owner: But you said you'd never had an accident.

Jockey: Yes sir. He did it on purpose.

At an elegant London ball a young lady and gentleman were dancing. 'They say I'm the best dancer in the country,' simpered the affected young female. 'You may be the best dancer in the country,' said the man, as his feet were trodden on yet again, 'but you don't seem to be when you're in town.'

Little Johnny was told by his teacher to write a full account of any cricket match he'd seen. The next day, the pedagogue was shocked to find just three words in Johnny's exercise book. 'Rain stopped play.'

'Waiter, what on earth is this you've just given me?'

'It's bean soup, sir.'

'I'm not interested in what it's been – I want to know what it is now!'

McTavish, a devout church elder, had never been to a race meeting before, but one day his friend McDougal persuaded him to go with him. He got McTavish to bet one pound on a horse which came in at

100-1. As the cashier paid out the pile of winnings, McTavish said in astonishment to McDougal, 'Ye mean tae say I get all this for a poond? Jings man, how long has this been going on?!'

McDougal had a great idea for saving on cab fares. At Queen Street station he saw a man get in a taxi and heard him ask for a street close to his own. McDougal jumped in and sat on the seat next to him. 'Hello there,' said the canny Scot, holding out his hand in greeting. 'Mah name's McDougal.' 'Mine, sir,' replied the passenger, 'is *not*.'

'Dad warned me not to go to adult cinemas in case I saw something I shouldn't see there. He was right – I saw him.'

Wife: It says on this medical report you've fathered two children. But we've only got one.
Husband: Er – I think it was a secretarial error.

'How's it going with your new girlfriend?'
'She broke it off.'
'Better luck next time.'
'Yes...assuming the stitches hold.'

Other humour titles
from Montpelier Publishing

The Old Fashioned Joke Book

The Book of Church Jokes

After Dinner Laughs

After Dinner Laughs 2

Scottish Jokes

Welsh Jokes

Jewish Jokes

Medical Jokes

Non-Corny Knock Knock Jokes

The Father Christmas Joke Book for Kids

Wedding Jokes

A Little Book of Limericks

Take my Wife! Hilarious Jokes of Love and Marriage

   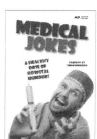

Printed in Great Britain
by Amazon